BEYOND
THE CATECHIST'S
TOOLBOX

Other Loyola Press Books by Joe Paprocki

The Catechist's Toolbox: How to Thrive as a Religious Education Teacher

La caja de herramientas del catequista: Cómo triunfar en el ministerio de la catequesis

The Bible Blueprint: A Catholic's Guide to Understanding and Embracing God's Word

Los Planos de la Biblia: Una quía católica para entender y acoger la palabra de Dios

Living the Mass: How One Hour a Week Can Change Your Life (with Fr. Dominic Grassi)

Vivir la misa: Cómo una hora a la semana puede combiar tu vida (with Fr. Dominic Grassi)

Practice Makes Catholic: Moving from a Learned Faith to a Lived Faith

7 Keys to Spiritual Wellness: Enriching Your Faith by Strengthening the Health of Your Soul

A Well-Built Faith: A Catholic's Guide to Knowing and Sharing What We Believe

Una fe bien construida: Guía católica para conocer y compartir lo que creemo

Beyond the Catechist's Toolbox

Catechesis That Not Only Informs but Also Transforms

Joe Paprocki, DMin

LOYOLA PRESS.
A JESUIT MINISTRY
Chicago

LOYOLA PRESS.
A JESUIT MINISTRY

3441 N. Ashland Avenue
Chicago, Illinois 60657
(800) 621-1008
www.loyolapress.com

In accordance with c. 827, permission to publish is granted on
October 12, 2012 by Rev. Msgr. John F. Canary, Vicar General of the
Archdiocese of Chicago. Permission to publish is an official declaration of
ecclesiastical authority that the material is free from doctrinal and moral
error. No legal responsibility is assumed by the grant of this permission.

"Called to Holiness" from *Finding God: Our Response to God's Gifts* Grade 5
Catechist Guide (Loyola Press, 2013). All rights reserved. Used with permission.

Art Credits: © iStockphoto.com/shorrocks, © iStockphoto.com/ivanastar,
© iStockphoto.com/Pixlmaker, Thinkstock/iStockphoto, Kathryn Seckman
Kirsch, AgnusImages.com

Library of Congress Cataloging-in-Publication Data
Paprocki, Joe.
  Beyond the catechist's toolbox : catechesis that not only informs, but also
transforms / by Joe Paprocki, DMin.
      pages cm
  ISBN-13: 978-0-8294-3829-1
  ISBN-10: 0-8294-3829-7
1. Catechetics—Catholic Church. I. Title.
  BX1968.P375 2013
  268'.82—dc23

                                                            2012040757

Printed in the United States of America.
13 14 15 16 17 18 RRD 10 9 8 7 6 5 4 3 2 1

I dedicate this book to one of the finest catechists I ever had the pleasure of knowing, the late Miguel Arias. I miss you, mi amigo.

Contents

Introduction

In 2005, I introduced *The Catechist's Toolbox: How to Thrive as a Religious Education Teacher* (Loyola Press). Since then, tens of thousands of catechists have benefited from the tools and tips I shared in that book for becoming a more effective catechist. Now it's time to take it to the next level!

The Catechist's Toolbox is chock-full of ideas and strategies designed to help catechists—most of whom are not professional teachers—get acclimated to the world of teaching. Armed with the tools to master their role, many catechists soon realize that teaching the Catholic faith is so much more than passing along information. As they enter more deeply into the catechetical experience, they realize that they are encountering a mystery. They also realize that guiding their learners into this mystery requires another skill set altogether.

This book, *Beyond the Catechist's Toolbox: Catechesis That Not Only Informs but Also Transforms,* builds on the foundation laid in *The Catechist's Toolbox* by helping catechists take their catechesis "up a notch" so that it reaches learners and participants at a deeper level.

My prayer is that this book will assist you in helping those you teach encounter the risen Christ in their midst, transforming their minds and hearts so that they will live as true disciples. May God grant us the grace we need to proclaim his living Word so that it might be heard!

Joe Paprocki, DMin, The Feast of St. Ignatius
Loyola, July 31, 2012

Chapter 1

How Can the Gospel Be Boring?

"This is boring!"

These three words, when spoken by young people in religious education classes, can break a catechist's heart. How on earth can the Gospel of Jesus be boring? We catechists certainly don't find the Gospel boring. In fact, we are on fire with the Word of God and can't wait to share it with others and set their hearts on fire. It can be very frustrating and downright disheartening to have young people react to our proclamation of the Gospel with a yawn. If we ourselves are on fire and the message we are teaching is "hot stuff," then it stands to reason that the fault must lie in one other place: our method of delivery. After all, whether we like it or not, *the medium is the message.*

This expression, coined in the mid-twentieth century by Marshall McLuhan, an educator, philosopher, and communications expert, tells us that a message and the manner in which it is conveyed are inseparable; the "packaging" in which a message is delivered shapes the message itself and adds to—or detracts from—its meaning. Therefore, if those we teach are bored, it is most likely because our methods are not engaging. We may be draining meaning from God's message without intending to.

Let me give you an example. When I was a kid, I spent hours watching baseball on TV. It just so happens that the two Chicago baseball teams—the White Sox and the Cubs—were not only on different sides of the city and on different TV channels, but also they were on completely different TV frequencies. Beginning in 1968, the Chicago White Sox games were no longer broadcast on VHF TV (the band of channels from 1 to 13) but on UHF TV (the band of channels above 13). The result was a picture with terrible reception. I no longer found White Sox games interesting because the fuzzy picture interfered with the excitement of the game. To this day, I believe poor TV reception was one of the main reasons I became a Cubs fan. (It certainly wasn't because the Cubs were winning any championships!) The excitement of baseball came through crystal clear on Cubs' broadcasts and engaged my youthful imagination, while White Sox games seemed boring.

In the same way, the problem for us catechists is not with the message we are delivering. Nor is there a problem with us; our hearts are in the right place. The problem is with our method of delivery, which, for many learners, feels like just another class period in a long school day.

The Same Old, Same Old

Much of our classroom approach to catechesis can be summed up in a three-word phrase: *reading the textbook*. Often, catechetical sessions consist of students taking turns reading aloud sentences or paragraphs from the textbook and catechists interjecting comments and questions for discussion. Yawn, right?

The problem is not with the textbook itself, however. Thank goodness for textbooks! Where would we catechists be without them? These wonderful books bring the richness and depth of our Catholic faith and heritage to life. The words and images proclaim the Gospel in ways appropriate to young people of various ages. The catechist's manuals provide us with a clear and concise understanding of the curriculum that we are responsible for transmitting.

The problem is that we are using the textbook as though it were the one and only resource at our disposal. If catechesis were simply about *information*, this would not be a problem. We could give the textbooks to our young people, have them digest the contents, and test them on their comprehension. However, catechesis is about more than information. It is about *transformation*.

When we limit catechesis to the acquisition of information, we reduce it to a subject like all the other subjects young people study in school. Religious education gets crammed inside the locker of a young person's mind right along with social studies, science, history, and math. We catechists, however, are not teachers of a subject. We are facilitators of an encounter—an encounter with a living God: Father, Son, and Holy Spirit. The church teaches us that the purpose of catechesis is to "put people not only in touch, but also in communion and intimacy, with

Jesus Christ" (*General Directory for Catechesis*, 80). As we all know, intimacy is not achieved by reading a book.

Before we go any further, however, let me be crystal clear that the textbook plays a crucial role in the catechetical process. And I'm not just saying that because I work for a publisher of catechetical textbooks. The fact is, when I teach, I most definitely and regularly use the textbook and catechist's manual. However, I would venture to say that we spend no more than 20 percent of our time in my sessions reading from the textbook. The other 80 percent of the time is spent engaging in experiences that bring the information from the textbook to life, that is, teaching beyond the book.

Teaching Beyond the Book

In this book, we are going to explore how to catechize beyond the textbook, but we aren't going to discard it. Likewise, we are going to catechize beyond the "toolbox" I provided in *The Catechist's Toolbox,* but we are not going to discard those tools. On the contrary, we are going to use the textbook and the "toolbox" as foundations on which to build a catechetical session that is an experience of transformation.

To find the key to teaching beyond the book, we can once again look to the *General Directory for Catechesis,* which reminds us that when "catechesis is permeated by a climate of prayer, the assimilation of the entire Christian life reaches its summit" (85). In other words, the most effective catechesis takes place in a prayerful environment. Why? Because prayer is an encounter with the living God.

Reading a textbook helps us know *about* God. Prayer helps us *know* God. Both are needed. Knowing about someone can help us know him or her better, and the better we know someone, the more we may want to learn about him or her. Teaching beyond the book works in a similar way. It makes God's presence palpable and tangible, which makes the learner long for more. In the pages ahead, we will explore a number of practical, creative, and effective ways for you to engage those you teach and help them encounter God's presence in their lives, leading to a transformation of mind and heart and an intimate relationship with Jesus Christ.

Chapter 2

More Like Mass Than Class

Recently, I spent a good deal of time researching my ancestry in preparation for a big family reunion. I uncovered story after story of forefathers and fore-mothers who came to the shores of the United States from Poland in the late nineteenth century. I was particularly impressed with the story of my maternal great-great-grandmother, Julia—who spoke seven languages fluently—making her transition to the new world, and Chicago in particular, so much easier.

Whenever we spend time in a country where another language is spoken, it behooves us to learn that language. Doing so makes us more capable of encountering others and developing relationships, be they social or professional. Catechesis is no differ-ent. In a very real sense, it is the process of inviting someone to enter into a new place—a "foreign land," so to speak. The foreign land is the kingdom of God. For many of those we teach, this land is strange and new. Its inhabitants act differently, think differently, and live differently. They speak differently, too; and to help our students enter this new reality, we must teach them its native language. Not only is it a language of love, but it's also a language of mystery—one that often transcends words.

In fact, in the kingdom of God, words are not the primary form of expression. The inhabitants of the kingdom of God are more at home with a language that relies less on an alphabet and more on expressions that speak to and prod the imagination. So, just what are the elements of this language of mystery? Let's take a quick look.

Sign and Symbol

In the kingdom of God, a type of sign language is spoken. Think about how Moses was drawn to encounter God—not through a wordy invitation but through the sign of a burning bush. Upon seeing this sign, Moses said, "I must go over and see this." Signs and symbols speak directly to the heart, through the imagination. They invite rather than command, and inspire rather than explain.

Ritual

In the kingdom of God, rituals abound. They connect us with meaningful events in our past, they ground us in the present, and they lead us confidently into the future. Rituals awaken a deeper level of consciousness within us. They remind us that we are truly at home in that special place where the spirit dwells.

Movement and Gesture

In the kingdom of God, people are often on the move—not mindlessly, like hamsters on a wheel, but intentionally, like dancers on a stage. They move about prayerfully, as though each movement is saying something. This notion is not foreign to us. A popular form of gentle exercise is tai chi, an ancient practice that promotes serenity through controlled movements that connect body, mind, and spirit. What happens to one affects the other. This is true in the kingdom of God, too: when we use our bodies for prayerful movement and gesture, the mind hears, and the heart responds.

Silence

In the kingdom of God, the primary form of expression is silence. Thomas Keating, a Trappist monk, tells us that "Silence is God's first language; everything else is a poor translation. In order to hear that language, we must learn to be still and to rest in God" (*Invitation to Love*).

Song

The kingdom of God is a place where the music never stops. Few things can touch our hearts and transport our minds better than music and song. This must be why the psalms refer to music so often—almost a hundred times, in fact. "O sing to the Lord a new song," the psalmist urges us (96:1). Lucky for us, God loves music, and he loves to hear us sing.

Story and Myth

In the kingdom of God, it is always story time. Approximately one-third of the recorded sayings of Jesus take the form of parables. The man could tell a story! He knew that stories create worlds—new realities that we can envision and enter into. Jesus' stories tap into our imaginations, compelling us to consider the possibility of an alternate reality. Author John Shea tells us that "story is the most interesting and compelling of language forms" and that "storytelling raises us out of the randomness of the moment and inserts us into a larger framework" (*Stories of Faith*). That larger framework is the kingdom of God, and we all have a part to play in it.

The language of mystery that is spoken in the kingdom of God predisposes us to the possibility of an alternate reality. The kingdom of God is, in fact, an alternate reality embedded within the one we can see and hear. We are called to enter into this reality by training our eyes, ears, and spirits to perceive the world anew. Knowing the language of mystery can help us answer the call. This is what catechesis is all about. If things were simply as they appeared, we would have no need for catechesis. However, life's ultimate meaning is veiled and mysterious. As such, we catechize others to incorporate these various elements of the language of mystery into their souls' daily diet.

So, where and when in the life of a Catholic is this language best spoken and heard? In the liturgy, of course. When we celebrate the Mass—or any of the sacraments, for that matter—we speak and are spoken to through a language of mystery.

The Language of Mystery

Elements	Examples
Signs and symbols	Water, oil, fire, bread, wine, and incense
Rituals	Sprinkling rites, anointings, and blessings
Movements and gestures	The Sign of the Cross, processions, and the sign of peace
Silence	Before Mass, after the Scripture readings, after the homily, and after Communion
Song	Hymns of the Mass and sung parts of Mass
Story and myth	The Liturgy of the Word

The language of mystery permeates Mass. And yet, for some reason, when we enter the realm of catechesis, we are suddenly at a loss for the nonverbal. The language of mystery is forgotten, and we revert to words, words, words.

Wordiness tends to reign in catechetical settings. Unfortunately, wordiness does not reign in the Reign of God! For these reasons, I can't emphasize enough the fact that *our catechesis should be more like Mass than class.*

I've been using this idea in my *Catechist's Toolbox* presentations for many years, and it never fails to provoke interest. I usually expand the idea by introducing the various elements of the language of mystery—signs, rituals, and so on—and encouraging catechists to incorporate them into their catechetical settings. Time and again, however, catechists have responded with frustration, saying, "I want to do this, but how can I when I have so much material to cover?"

One way we *can't* do it is by cramming elements of the language of mystery into an existing lesson plan. Instead, we must deliver the content by "translating" it into the language of mystery. We will still rely on and incorporate words, of course, but at the same time we will be speaking in a language that transcends words. We will be speaking in a language of mystery that not only informs, but also transforms!

With these goals in mind, I began offering another workshop that went beyond *The Catechist's Toolbox* and offered an approach to catechesis that incorporates the language of mystery. In my ongoing efforts to be as practical as possible—to offer something that really works—I developed a Template for Worshipful Catechesis. This template outlines a seventy-five-minute catechetical session that incorporates the various elements of the language of mystery as a prayerful context within which the textbook content is delivered. The response has been incredible. Catechists are eagerly embracing this approach, transitioning to a model of catechesis that not only informs, but also transforms.

What follows is that template, organized into five stages for a seventy-five-minute session:

1. Preliminaries (15 minutes)
2. The ENGAGE Step (15 minutes)
3. The EXPLORE Step (25 minutes)

4. The REFLECT Step (10 minutes)

5. The RESPOND Step (10 minutes)

Together, these steps form what we refer to as the "catechetical process." No matter what textbook you are using, its lessons are most likely arranged in steps—sometimes three, sometimes four. For the purposes of this book, I have elected to use the four-step process employed by the *Finding God* series (Loyola Press). I am doing so for two reasons. First, this is the program used in the parish where I teach, so I actually follow these four steps. Second, these four steps include a significant segment for prayer—the Reflect step.

In catechesis, prayer needs to be more than just a couple of brief bookends used to open and close the session. A prayer experience is critical if we are seeking an encounter with the risen Christ. Occasionally, a concerned catechist will say to me, "I'd like to be able to include a prayer experience in my lesson, but I have so much content to get through." In response, I point out that prayer is a key part of the content we are delivering. Along with the Creed, the Sacraments, and the Moral Life, Prayer is one of the four pillars of the *Catechism of the Catholic Church.* Without this fourth pillar, we are inviting our learners to step onto a table that has only three legs. Delivering content about Jesus without talking to and spending time with Jesus is teaching "just" a subject. And remember, we are doing much more than that.

So, without further adieu, let's explore how we can invite young people into the kingdom of God by using its language—the language of mystery.

Chapter 3

Preliminaries

15 Minutes

Every catechist knows that if a session is scheduled to last seventy-five minutes, only about sixty of those minutes will be spent actually teaching. Why? Because there are preliminaries to deal with: roll call, late arrivals, the collection of paperwork, the distribution of materials, requests to use the restroom, and the eternal challenge of getting young people to settle in and focus.

The first ten to fifteen minutes of a session don't have to be completely devoid of teaching, however. We catechists can use a variety of strategies to make the most of this preliminary period—to teach while we are busy doing things that don't feel like teaching. For this to happen, though, we must embrace the notion I proposed earlier: our session should feel *more like Mass and less like class.* With this key idea in mind, let's take a look at some of the ways a catechist can use the preliminary period to set the tone for a worshipful and prayerful experience.

Greeting Participants with Holy Water

What's one of the first things you do when you enter a Catholic church? You dip your fingers into a holy-water font or receptacle and then bless yourself. This is a powerful reminder that, through the waters of baptism, we have died to sin and risen to new life in Christ. Why not invite your participants to enter your learning space in the same way? This can be done very easily.

Acquire a small glass bowl with a lid that seals tightly. Fill the bowl with holy water from the stoup, or dispenser, in your parish church. Bring this bowl to each session or find a place to store it in your learning space. A few minutes before your session is scheduled to begin, stand at the entrance with the bowl of holy water and invite participants to bless themselves as they arrive. Better yet, have an aide or a reliable student assume "holy-water duty" so that you are free to continue with your preliminaries.

This ritual—an element of the language of mystery—will signal to participants that they are entering a sacred space. It will also put them in touch with a welcoming human face, one of the most powerful expressions of God's presence. Participants will recognize the ritual as an act of worship performed when entering a church. Even if they don't realize it on a conscious level, their minds and hearts will start to turn toward God.

Play Liturgical Music as Participants Arrive

When we enter a church, our senses are immediately stimulated. We see stained-glass windows, statues, and flowers. We smell candles and incense. We put our fingers into holy water and genuflect before entering our pew. And we hear music. Sometimes the choir or organist is rehearsing that day's Mass music or playing background music to help us transition to worship. I suggest you offer the same auditory experience for your participants as they arrive.

Bring a CD player or MP3 player to your learning space, or arrange for one to be available. Play inspirational music softly in the background to set the tone for participants as they arrive, and keep the music playing until it is time to conduct business. You might experiment with traditional Catholic hymns, instrumental music, or contemporary Christian music, or ask your catechetical leader for suggestions or links to music that is appropriate. You might select a song that reinforces the theme of the lesson and have it play on a loop so that the melody becomes familiar to your participants. Over time, you might find yourself building your own library of music for use in your faith formation sessions.

The phrase "to sing" (and its variations) appears over 300 times in Scripture. When we want to approach God, spoken words alone do not suffice. Playing music as participants enter your learning space will introduce them to the language of mystery and to the idea that they are entering into something sacred—something that will touch them at a deeper level than words alone.

Invite Participants to Write
Prayer Intentions

Tradition invites us to kneel and pray when we arrive in church. Many of us use this time to tell God what is weighing on our hearts and minds. We don't "check our baggage" at the door as we enter a church. Rather, we bring it with us and offer it to God. In the same way, you can invite your participants to develop the habit of engaging in prayer the moment they take a seat.

Place an index card and a pen or pencil at each place before participants arrive. As they get settled, direct participants to write a prayer intention for the week. The intention might be a prayer of thanksgiving, an expression of wonder or praise, or a request for help. You can either have participants keep their cards to use in the opening prayer or invite them to place the cards in a basket on the prayer table.

Getting in touch with their own gratitude, needs, and feelings of awe will help prepare your participants to encounter our loving God. Naming our joys helps us develop an attitude of gratitude that acknowledges God as the source of all blessings. Naming our needs helps us remember our dependence on something greater than ourselves. And even the simplest words of praise remind us that we are creatures made for worship and for song.

Taking Attendance and Doing Business

As previously noted, every catechist has what feels like a million and one things to do at the start of class: taking attendance, distributing materials, addressing questions, and so on. The suggestions I've offered thus far will not interfere with your ability to accomplish these things. Instead, they may even facilitate the process by creating a prayerful, restful environment. While participants are entering, signing themselves with holy water, hearing music, and writing prayers, you can be taking care of business. The beauty of it is that through these actions, you will be teaching without even trying to.

Procession to Set the Prayer Table

Once everyone is seated and you have had an opportunity to conduct preliminary business, it's time to invite your participants into another prayerful experience: a procession to set up the prayer table.

Processions are a sacramental; they represent the spiritual journey that we're all on, and they remind us of our ultimate destination—to be with God.

As I noted in *The Catechist's Toolbox,* a prayer center can be a simple table draped with a cloth whose color reflects the liturgical season; on it might be placed a Bible and a crucifix, a statue, an icon, or another religious object. Such a space demonstrates the value of prayer and builds an awareness of the sacred. To deepen this awareness, you can invite participants to come to the table prayerfully and prepare it for your time together in a number of ways. Here is one approach.

1. Invite participants to bring their own symbols to add to the prayer table during your first few sessions. Point out that these can be religious symbols such as crosses or holy cards, or objects that remind participants of God in less obvious ways—birthday cards, flowers, or photos of loved ones, for example.

2. Before the procession, invite participants to line up along one side of the room, holding either an item from the prayer table (including

the cloth, the Bible, and the other sacred objects) or a new item they've brought with them that day.

3. Have an aide or a reliable participant lead the procession, holding a cross that will be placed on the table.

4. Play music as participants process around the perimeter of the room and arrive at the prayer table.

5. Have participants place their objects on the prayer table one by one, beginning with the cloth, the cross, and the Bible, and followed by the other objects and symbols.

6. Invite participants to return to their places quietly and prayerfully.

Instead of rushing to set up the prayer table on your own before the session begins, consider inviting your participants to set it up as described here. In doing so, you will be teaching them reverence and sacramentality—two key elements of the language of mystery. And on a more practical note, the entire procession should last no more than a few minutes. What do you have to lose?

Opening Prayer

Now that the prayer table is set, you are ready for an opening prayer experience. This prayer can take many forms. I recommend the following.

1. Invite participants to stand. Standing is the traditional posture for prayer. (Have you ever noticed how the congregation stands whenever the priest says, "Let us pray"?)

2. Pray the Sign of the Cross.

3. Continue with a call-and-response greeting that you can teach participants over the first few weeks. Here are some possibilities.

Call	**Response**
This is the day the Lord has made.	*Let us rejoice and be glad!*
Lord, send out your Spirit,	*and renew the face of the earth.*
Our help is in the name of the Lord,	*who made heaven and earth.*
O Lord, come to my aid.	*O Lord, make haste to help me.*
O Lord, open my lips,	*and my mouth shall declare your praise.*

4. Invite participants to make the threefold Sign of the Cross with their thumb on the forehead, lips, and chest. Initiate this by saying, "*Let's pray today that God's Word will be* . . . in our minds [forehead], on our lips [lips], and in our hearts [chest]."

5. After several weeks introduce the gesture by using only the italicized words above.

6. Invite participants to share a prayer intention. Pass around a candle (battery operated if necessary) and have participants either pray their own intention aloud or take one from the prayer basket and read it aloud.

7. Conclude the opening prayer by inviting participants to pray aloud a traditional prayer.

8. Consider changing the traditional prayer monthly, especially if there are prayers you wish your participants to learn.

By beginning your session in this prayerful manner, you will help participants adopt a more reverent attitude toward the catechetical experience. At the same time, you will teach them about ritual prayer, sacramental gestures, intercessory prayer, and traditional prayer.

You're Now Ready to "Begin" Teaching

At this point, you may feel as though you are finally ready to begin teaching. The truth is that you have been teaching throughout this preliminary period. Isn't that nice to know? Instead of allowing participants to arrive on their own terms and enter into a chaotic atmosphere like recess before the bell, you have set the tone for a sacred experience in which they will encounter the presence of the living God. The stage is now set to move into a more formal experience of teaching and learning—all of it within the context and climate of prayer that you have established during this preliminary period.

Congratulations!

Chapter 4

The ENGAGE Step

10 Minutes

Make no mistake about it: you've already done some important teaching if you incorporated any of the Preliminaries strategies into the first fifteen minutes of your session. Even if you were busy taking attendance and getting last-minute details into place, the climate of prayer you've already established (using holy water, background music, prayer intentions, and so on) has clearly communicated to your participants that what happens here will be an encounter with mystery.

Now it's time to embark on the actual lesson for the day. This step of the catechetical process can be referred to as the Engage step: in it, we seek to capture the imaginations of our participants and introduce our focus for the lesson. The goal of this step is to "hook" your participants with an image or idea from their lived experience—something they can relate to—that is also associated with the session topic. To better understand this concept, let's turn to a master catechist, St. Ignatius of Loyola, who taught over 500 years ago but is still relevant today.

Entering Through Their Door

St. Ignatius of Loyola taught the Catholic faith in the face of the great challenges presented by the Protestant Reformation in the sixteenth century. He trained his followers, the Jesuits, to use special techniques to win over audiences. (Ignatius was a soldier by trade, so he knew a few things about tactics.) One of the first strategies he taught was the concept of "entering through their door—but leaving through your own." Ignatius knew that the most effective way to engage an audience is to capture their imaginations with an experience from daily living—something familiar, easily recognizable. More than likely, he got this idea from Jesus himself, the ultimate teacher. Jesus consistently taught by entering through the door of his listeners, engaging their imaginations and then challenging them to consider the reality of the kingdom of God. The images he used were simple and very familiar to first-century Palestinians (and to us, for that matter). Here a few of them.

- a mustard seed
- yeast
- a treasure hidden in a field
- a net
- a pearl
- a wedding feast
- wheat and weeds
- a father who had two sons
- a shepherd and a lost sheep
- blindness
- a light and a bushel
- a lost coin

It makes perfect sense that Jesus would use images like these to "enter through his listeners' door." After all, he entered through our "door" in the very act of becoming human. Through familiar images, Jesus ventured into the everyday lives of everyday people to reveal the reality of the kingdom of God in their midst. At the same time, he *was* the kingdom of God in their midst. As the stories and images entered his listeners' imaginations, so did he.

For these reasons, we catechists do well to follow Jesus' teaching example and that of St. Ignatius of Loyola. Let's take a closer look at how we can engage those we teach by entering through their door so that they may leave through Christ's.

What's the Big Idea?

I once took a course in homiletics (the art of delivering homilies and liturgical reflections). The professor often said, "Unless you can summarize the goal of your homily in one sentence, you have no business being in the pulpit." He was serious about that. When we got up to deliver a practice homily, we were asked to tell the class our main goal in a single sentence. If we couldn't, he made us sit down.

Surely the same advice applies to catechists: unless we can summarize in a single sentence the goal or theme of our lesson, we have no business teaching the class. As you do your planning, then, a good question to ask yourself is "What's the Big Idea?" Once you know what your one-sentence Big Idea is, you'll be able to announce it to your participants and return to it over and over throughout the lesson. Think of it this way. When a parent asks "What did you learn today?" on the way home from class, the student should be able to state the Big Idea without missing a beat. (And imagine how happy the parent will be to hear something other than "nothin'" or "I dunno"!)

Marketing experts abide by a principle known as the Rule of Seven. According to this principle, a member of a target audience must see or hear a message at least seven times before it "sinks in" and compels him or her to act on it. Without this repetition, the message gets lost among competing messages. The audience doubts that the product or service is truly needed. There is concern about cost and uncertainty that the seller can be trusted. A catechist's aims are a little different; we're not trying to sell something for a profit, for example. But still, the Rule of Seven comes in handy, because, in a sense, we are "marketing God." We are striving to convey an idea we consider essential to our students' lives and well-being. We are also up against many competing messages. Our participants are not yet convinced that they really need the Gospel of Jesus to live happily and successfully. They are also concerned about the "cost" of discipleship. And finally, they are not altogether sure that they trust us. Building that trust takes time. Therefore, we need to announce our Big Idea boldly, clearly, and often.

So, where does the Big Idea come from? In most cases, we can find it stated clearly in our catechist's manual. Often, the Big Idea is expressed in the chapter or lesson title, which strongly relates to the session's theme. For example, when I flip randomly through my Grade 6 *Finding God* catechist's manual, I find the following Big Ideas, or themes:

1. Session 3: The root of sin is lack of trust in God.
2. Session 12: The Psalms help us to learn how to pray.
3. Session 16: The prophets called people to repentance and conversion.
4. Session 21: Jesus calls us to practice the virtues of faith, hope, and charity.

Once we identify a session's Big Idea and can say it in a single sentence, we need to plan ahead to "publicize" it throughout the session. How do we do this? We can write it on the board in big, bold letters before class. We can print it on any handouts being used that session. We can include it in PowerPoint presentations we might give. We can state it repeatedly throughout the lesson, and we can refer to it in our prayer experiences. We can select and play music that reinforces it. We can have our students design posters or write essays or draw pictures that express it. Like any good marketing strategist, we can search for and use as many clever and effective ways of announcing our message as possible.

Most importantly, once you have a clear idea of your session's Big Idea, you can use it to "enter through their door."

How to "Hook 'Em"

There are infinite "doorways" into your students' minds and hearts. The key to the Engage step is finding the one that best relates to the Big Idea you are teaching. This doorway will be marked with an image or idea that is familiar and interesting to your students. For example, the Big Idea of a fourth-grade session I once taught was "God shapes our conscience." I focused on the word *shape*—since it was the most vivid—and asked myself how this word related to the life of a fourth-grader. Before long, I had landed on the image of shaping clay. I went to the store and picked up some small canisters of Play-Doh and then distributed them during the Engage step of the session. After inviting the children to make shapes, I walked about, encouraging and affirming their creations and repeatedly using the word *shape* as I did so. (When I commented that I used to enjoy Play-Doh as a kid, one student answered, "They had it back then?" Wise guy.)

After a few minutes, I invited my little sculptors to share what they had made. After show-and-tell, I talked about the nature of clay itself. I pointed out that we can shape Play-Doh only if it remains fresh and pliable. Then I asked what happens if it's left uncovered. The experts responded that it hardens and becomes impossible to shape.

Now it was time to make the big segue. I said, "Today we're going to learn about how God can shape us, especially that part of us we call our conscience. As long as we stay under God's protection, our hearts will remain easy to shape. When we stray from God, our hearts can harden and become more difficult to shape." In a minute or less, I had entered through their door and started moving them toward mine—and God's. The stage was now set to learn how God does indeed shape our conscience.

About a month after that session, the associate pastor visited the classroom and asked the question all catechists dread: "So, boys and girls, what have you been learning?" I crossed my fingers and prayed silently that the kids would have something to say. A few of them shared thoughts about that evening's lesson, and one or two recalled something from previous weeks. This was followed by the sound of crickets. After waiting for what seemed like an eternity, I prodded the children: "Somebody tell Father about Play-Doh." The kids seemed puzzled at first, but then one girl raised her hand and proudly announced, "God can shape our conscience." Thank you, Jesus!

What I found interesting was that the girl didn't say a word about Play-Doh. What she did remember was the Big Idea from that lesson—exactly as I had hoped. She had walked through the door of Play-Doh, toward the door that leads to Christ.

What About Older Kids?

Of course, entering through the door of a fourth grader is different from entering the door of a junior high student. Let's consider this difference by way of example.

Once, when teaching eighth graders, I was planning a session with the following Big Idea: "We can trust God, our Father." I had decided that my focus would be on the concept of trust. If you know anything about teenagers, you know that they are wired—literally. They are constantly connected to some form of device, often listening to music. In fact, experts report that kids in this age group listen to music an average of three to three-and-a-half hours a day. There's no doubt about it: when you enter through the door of junior high kids, you find music. I had therefore made a consistent and concerted effort to find contemporary music that would hook their attention and engage their imaginations.

For this particular session, I found a song by a popular band in which the singer laments the fact that he can no longer trust someone who used to be close to him. After playing the song for my students, I asked them to describe the singer's emotions. They responded that he felt angry, frustrated, and betrayed. Next, I asked what the person must have done to make the singer feel that way. They guessed that the person had "stabbed him in the back" or been "two-faced." After discussing how hard it is to trust someone in such circumstances, I asked the young people to name the person they trust most. Some named a friend; others a family member, a teacher, or a coach. Then, in a moment of real honesty, one young man said, "No one. Only me."

When it happens, you know it. I had entered through this young man's door, into a world where trust does not come easy. And the other young people had followed. We were now in a sacred place, together.

Once I became aware of this fact, I was able to make the segue and introduce the Big Idea. "Trust can be very hard," I said. "It's especially hard to trust people if they've let us down. Today we're going to learn about trusting God, our Father. We can trust God because he has always kept his promise to be faithful to us—especially in sending us his Son, Jesus Christ."

It was time to put the CD player away and usher my students from their door to mine. The remainder of the lesson was spent exploring the story of our salvation and how, even though God's people are often unfaithful, God remains faithful and never lets his people down. The young people left the session, armed with an important Big Idea: God the Father can indeed be trusted.

No Loitering

An important thing to keep in mind when "entering through their door" is that we don't want to loiter on the threshold. The goal is to step in, take a look around, select and focus on one image, and then bring that image along as you lead participants toward your door. This can be difficult, since young people love to tell their own stories—and, dare I say it, dwell on themselves. But keeping things in motion is crucial. It communicates that you've got somewhere important to go. Over time, and little by little, those you teach will begin to see that their everyday experience points directly to God. They will begin to know at a very deep level that God is involved in their everyday lived experience and that, as St. Ignatius taught, God can be found in all things.

Now that you've engaged your learners, it's time to share with them the riches of our faith heritage and open them up to God's presence in their lives. Let's Explore.

Chapter 5

The EXPLORE Step

25 Minutes

Up to this point, you've established a prayerful climate and introduced the Big Idea. Now it's time to deliver it: to show how the Big Idea, drawn from our faith heritage, sheds light on our daily living and transforms us—if we allow it to. In other words, you are about to pass on the content of our faith. What you've done in previous steps ensures that this content is not delivered in a vacuum. Rather, it will be handed on within a climate of prayer and in relation to lived experience. The task of the Explore step is to tie it all together—to show how our own individual stories are intimately linked to the "big story" of our salvation in Jesus Christ.

But First, More Prayer

Before you jump right into the textbook, however, there are a couple of things you can do to enhance the climate of prayer you've already created. Remember: your session should resemble Mass more than class.

A Moment of Silence

Reading a textbook about Jesus Christ and his Good News should be different from reading any other kind of textbook. It should be a sacred experience. To send a message that this reading is going to be something special, invite your participants to stand in silence for a few seconds. You might say "We're about to read from our book about the Good News that Jesus offers us. Let's prepare ourselves to open our minds and hearts to the Word of God by standing in silence for a few moments." If you've not yet invited participants to make the threefold Sign of the Cross on the forehead, lips, and heart, this would be an excellent time to do so, encouraging them to pray that the Word of God be in their minds, on their lips, and in their hearts. By doing this, you will be using sacred gesture (one of the elements of the language of mystery) to connect the Liturgy of the Word we celebrate at Mass and the reading of God's Word that's about to take place in your session.

A Reading from Scripture

Each lesson you teach has its basis in Scripture. This is why catechist's manuals from all major Catholic publishers include Scripture references for each lesson. These Scripture passages are usually brief, but are intimately connected with the Big Idea of your lesson. To remind your participants of this connection, invite a volunteer to come forward to proclaim the passage from the Bible.

- Be sure to bookmark the passage before your session.

- Make sure the Bible has been enthroned in a place of prominence (such as on the prayer table).

- Invite the volunteer to come forward, bow from the waist in front of the Bible as a sign of reverence, and pick up the Bible.

- After the passage is proclaimed, have the volunteer say "The Word of the Lord" (for readings other than Gospel readings) or "The Gospel of the Lord" (if the passage is from one of the four Gospels). Have the group respond accordingly with "Thanks be to God" or "Praise to you, Lord, Jesus Christ."

- Have the volunteer return the Bible to its place of honor, bow again in reverence, and return to his or her seat.

A Brief Review

This is a good time to review and reinforce concepts from the previous session. In his *Spiritual Exercises,* St. Ignatius of Loyola emphasized the need for repetition when learning and integrating new concepts, beliefs, and practices. This emphasis on repetition continues to be a hallmark of Ignatian pedagogy—teaching methods inspired by St. Ignatius. Repetition is not, however, the mindless recall of memorized material. Instead, it should consist of revisiting previously learned concepts to be able to build upon them and integrate them with new ones. Your review can be brief, and the connection between "last week" and "this week" can be simple—but it should be clear.

At last, it's time to have participants open their textbooks and learn more about the Big Idea you've been hinting at for thirty minutes or so.

Reading from the Textbook

At this point, you may be thinking, "All we've done so far is delay the boring part of the lesson." Not so. Reading from the textbook need not be boring—and it won't be if you've fashioned the type of environment we've described. In such an environment, textbook reading doesn't take place in a vacuum, unconnected from real life. Instead, it takes place in a climate of prayer—in the acknowledged and felt presence of the living God—and has a solid connection to everyday living.

Even so, it doesn't hurt to liven up the process. Here are some techniques for making classroom reading more active and less passive.

Ball Toss

You may have noticed that when you ask for volunteers to read aloud, a lot of heads drop and eyes look the other way. No one wants to volunteer. If so, try this: pull out a foam ball, toss it in the air, and then begin making arm motions as if throwing it toward the group. Hands will immediately go up to catch the ball, and many young people will beg you to toss it to them. In the midst of this frenzy, simply say, "OK, let's see who's going to read first," and then toss the ball to a reliable participant. Invite him or her to read as you normally would. Then, when it's time for the next student to read, tell the young person with the ball to toss it gently to another student. Like magic, the prospect of reading aloud will no longer deter the participants. They will all want the ball—and you will have a classroom full of volunteers.

Paired Interviews

This strategy works well when you have lots of material to read and your participants are in fourth grade or above. Arrange the students in pairs and assign half the text to one partner and half to the other. Explain that they should read their assigned text silently—and then give them less time than is humanly possible to complete the task. Why? To create a sense of urgency. If students begin to complain that, say, four minutes is not enough time, look at your watch and then respond with concern, "Now you have only three and a half minutes." Of course, if students need it, you can always tack on a little extra time when the "real" time is up. But make no mistake: you will have done yourself a favor by generating this sense of urgency.

After partners have read their sections silently and time has expired, invite them to take turns interviewing one another about the text. Provide an interview sheet with sample questions such as these: *What is the main idea of the section you read? What are the key words from this section? What is the most inspiring sentence or idea from this section? What is one idea from this section that all Catholics should know or do?* Once again, allow less time than is humanly possible. When all pairs are done with their interviews, invite students to share with the group what their partner read as you highlight and supplement important information.

Graphic Organizer

Give students a worksheet to help them identify and organize information as they read silently from the text. The graphic organizer should be simple. For example, it might be a sheet of paper with four empty boxes labeled *BIG Ideas, Key Words, Most Interesting Idea,* and *Huh?* When young people are done reading and recording ideas, you can use the graphic organizer to guide your follow-up discussion.

Clue Cards

Ahead of time, identify key words in the lesson text and write them on index cards, one word per card and at least one card per student—more if possible. During the Explore step of the session, distribute the cards to students. Explain that, as the text is being read aloud, they should yell "Time Out!" whenever they hear one of the words on their cards. When this happens, have the student show the card to the class, and then invite another student to explain the importance or the definition of the word. Amend or supply the student's answer as needed. You can tape the words up on the board to create a word wall for the lesson. If a student fails to call "Time Out!" when his or her clue word has been read, have that student stand for the remainder of the reading (or for an amount of time that seems reasonable).

There are many creative ways to read from a textbook, and these are just a few. The bottom line, though, is that a more active and less passive reading experience will reinforce an important idea in the minds of your participants: God deserves—and inspires—our energy and enthusiasm.

Reinforcement

The Mass that we celebrate is comprised of two main parts: the Liturgy of the Word and the Liturgy of the Eucharist. In essence, our worship consists of word and sign. We not only listen to God's Word, but we also participate in actions through which we more deeply encounter God's presence. In the same way, our catechetical sessions should strike a balance between word and action. After reading from the textbook, it's crucial that you reinforce the Big Idea by inviting your learners to participate in some type of activity.

I recommend an age-appropriate experience that helps your learners express, visualize, or otherwise experience the Big Idea. Chances are that your catechist's manual or publisher's Web site will suggest activities tied to each session's theme or Big Idea. Another great resource is the Activity Finder at www.loyolapress.com. (You need not be a user of a Loyola Press curriculum to access this resource; however, you will need to register as a member on the Web site.) Loyola Press also offers a product called *Expand the Experience,* a box that includes 120 laminated cards, each featuring an age-appropriate themed activity that will enhance an existing lesson in your program. All the activities do the following:

- Include adaptations for two different grade levels so that all children can participate, as well as inclusion suggestions that allow kids with special needs to join in the fun
- Fall under one of six themes—God, Jesus, the Church, the Sacraments, Morality, and the Seasons of the Church Year
- Engage children in active learning to reinforce the faith message and bring the lessons to life

Personally, I'm a big believer in activities that bring a lesson to life. In fact, I offer free "Getting Started as a Catechist" webinars on my blog, www.catechistsjourney.com, in which I identify and explain activities that are effective and appropriate for various age groups: primary, intermediate, junior high/high school, and adult. To view these in detail, visit my blog and look for the webinars tab at the top of the home page.

In the meantime, here are a few age-appropriate activities for various age groups.

Reinforcement Activities for Primary-Age Children

- Storytelling
- Drawing and making crafts
- Dramatizing
- Memorizing
- Singing
- Performing puppet shows
- Completing activity sheets or blackline masters

Reinforcement Activities for Intermediate-Age Children

- Doing hands-on activities and crafts
- Playing review games

- Reading independently (especially stories about Bible heroes)
- Singing
- Participating in group work or cooperative-learning activities
- Completing activity sheets or blackline masters
- Interacting with learning stations

Reinforcement Activities for Junior High and High School Students
- Listening and responding to contemporary music
- Using technology
- Staging debates and talk shows
- Playing ice-breaker games
- Designing props and visual aids
- Completing mature craft projects
- Discussing current events

Adult Catechesis

Catechists of adults have a very different role than do catechists of young people. Adult learners are self-directed; you don't have to hold their hands. The catechist of adults should view himself or herself as a facilitator rather than an authority—never forgetting, of course, that he or she has important information and experience to share. Adult participants should set the goals and timelines for their own learning experience; they want to have some sense of ownership of the process, and they're entitled to it. But just like young people, adults will learn best when they experience a desire to learn and when the reason for learning is clear. Therefore, it's important for the catechist to show why the material is valuable and how it connects with the participants' lived experience. After these things happen, the best reinforcement activity for adults is *conversation.*

Prayerful Transition

At the conclusion of the Explore step, it's time to transition into the segment of your session fully dedicated to prayer: the Reflect step. A good way to make this transition is to invite your participants to listen to (or join in singing) a song or hymn that expresses the session's Big Idea. Most major Catholic hymnals include an index that organizes hymns by theme. If you prefer high-tech research methods, the

Oregon Catholic Press Web site offers a list of key words (*charity, church, commandments, courage*), each of which is linked to a list of songs related to that topic—digital recordings included. Check it out at www.ocp.org/compositions/topics/10.

Once you've found a song or hymn you'd like to use, check with your catechetical leader to see if he or she has access to a recording of it, or download it from the Internet. You might also want to search for a visual meditation to accompany it; many are available on YouTube. When I typed in some randomly chosen hymn titles, for example ("One Bread, One Body," "I Am the Bread of Life," "Be Not Afraid," "Were You There?"), I found a range of quality reflections and meditations that were suitable for a catechetical setting.

Before you begin the Reflect step of the session, play the song and invite your learners to listen quietly or to sing along. When a prayerful mood has been set, you are ready to invite your participants into the most intimate segment of your session.

Chapter 6

The REFLECT Step

10 Minutes

It's time to enter into the most crucial step of the catechetical process: the moment we seek to encounter, in a very real way, the risen Christ who is in our midst. The Reflect step holds the key to differentiating what we do in catechesis from what teachers do in school. This step reminds us that Jesus Christ is not a subject but a living Person and that the goal of catechesis is to be in "communion and intimacy" with him (*General Directory for Catechesis* 80). The Reflect step is an intimate moment with Jesus.

Before we go any further, I want to point out two things about this step. First, kids can have a hard time adjusting to it—especially junior high kids. Second, kids of all ages quickly come to view it as their favorite part of the session. It may not be easy to teach young people to be still and quiet, but it is well worth the effort.

Using Our Imaginations to Pray

Catholic Tradition teaches us that, during her trial for heresy, St. Joan of Arc was ridiculed by the inquisitor. "You say God speaks to you," he taunted, "but it's only. your imagination." It is said that Joan courageously replied, "How else would God speak to me if not through my imagination?" St. Joan points out a very plain fact that many of us tend to overlook: God does indeed speak to us through our imaginations.

In his book *Touched by God*, Fr. John Powell, SJ, discusses how God speaks to us not so much through words, but through our feelings, memories, desires, thoughts, and ideas. In the Catholic Tradition, there is a long history of praying in such a way as to invite Jesus to speak to us through our imaginations. This type of prayer is called reflective prayer, and it is the kind of prayer experience that the Reflect step is designed to create.

Of course, one of the great champions of reflective prayer was St. Ignatius of Loyola. One of the many remarkable things about Ignatius was his incredible imagination. It was his own imagination that played a central role in his conversion and that continued to shape his prayer life throughout his ministry. In fact, his deep commitment to imaginative, or reflective, prayer has made this form of prayer one of the hallmarks of Ignatian spirituality.

Ignatius's approach to imaginative prayer encourages the individual to place himself or herself within a Gospel story and to use all the senses to participate in that story, paying close attention to what is seen, heard, smelled, felt, and even tasted. Above all, we are invited to pay close attention to what Jesus says in the Gospel story. Our imaginations are then equipped to hear what Jesus might be saying to *us*.

This type of prayer enables us to encounter Jesus in a very personal way—a way that brings Jesus into our hearts. It is therefore appropriate for people of all ages.

Three Steps

Leading guided reflections (or meditations) involves three basic steps:

1. Getting ready to pray
2. Leading the guided reflection
3. Allowing quiet time with God

The amount of time you should spend on a guided reflection depends on the age of your participants. A good rule of thumb is to spend one minute for every year of the participants' approximate age. If you are a preschool catechist, for example, you'll need to keep your guided reflection to about three or four minutes. (I've been told that about ninety seconds is ideal for this age group—but also that preschoolers love it and are "built" for it.) If you teach first to third graders, you will want to shoot for guided reflections of six to eight minutes. If you teach in the intermediate grades, ten minutes will be sufficient. With junior high or high school kids, you'll be able to approach the fifteen-minute mark. For adults, it is best to keep guided reflections in the fifteen- to twenty-minute range; anything longer can be challenging, no matter how old you are.

Let's take a closer look at the three basic steps for leading a guided reflection.

Step One: Getting Ready to Pray

Most people—especially kids—live busy, noisy lives and can't enter into a prayerful state on demand. A transition period is needed, and that's what this first step is all about. The goal is to invite your participants to focus on God's presence and to establish a quiet, prayerful, and comfortable mood to help them overcome distractions. This first step may take anywhere from thirty seconds for little ones to four or five minutes for older children and adults. Consider the following as you prepare your group for reflective prayer.

Suggest a Comfortable Posture

If possible, invite young people to move out of their seats and into a comfortable place on the floor where they can sit with their back straight against a wall. This posture gives the body support and keeps a person alert. I also like to invite participants to come forward and accept a small, battery-operated tea light—as a reminder of their baptism and the light of Christ—and carry it to their prayer spot, or "sacred space." (Over time, the kids begin referring to the entire guided-reflection experience as sacred space: "Mr. Paprocki, are we doing sacred space tonight?") If space is limited or if the floor is too hard, invite participants to get comfortable in their seats, perhaps spreading them out for "breathing room." Encourage participants to close their eyes or to focus their attention on a sacred symbol or picture.

Encourage Deep Breathing

Next, take a minute or two to help participants relax and breathe deeply. Ask them to relax their hands and to slowly and silently inhale, then gradually exhale. Help them establish a breathing rhythm by having them count slowly to three as they inhale and listen to you count softly to three as they exhale.

Use Reflective Music

Reflective or instrumental music can help by muting classroom distractions and softening the setting. For many, total silence is just too jarring.

Think of the music as white noise to fill in the background and create a relaxing and prayerful atmosphere. It works.

Step Two: Leading the Guided Reflection

Begin the guided reflection with an invitation to reflect or meditate on an aspect of the theme or Big Idea that you are teaching. Later we'll cover where your guided reflection may come from. Once you have it, here is a good way to use it.

Step-by-Step Directions

Through a series of age-appropriate directions that you have prepared or are following from a resource (such as a book of guided meditations for children, teens, or adults), invite participants to engage their imaginations and enter into a setting where they can encounter Jesus, dwell on his words, and converse with him.

Engage the Senses

Invite participants to use their imaginations to go to a place where they can encounter and speak with Jesus. The setting may be a favorite Scripture story (the birth of Jesus, the wedding at Cana, the Sermon on the Mount) or a favorite place, such as a field, a park, a beach, or a backyard. Invite participants to see, hear, smell, and feel the surroundings, and then initiate conversation with Jesus. Encourage them to talk to Jesus as they would to a very close friend.

Speak Slowly and Pause Often
By speaking slowly and pausing after each line of the reflection, you establish sacred space in which participants can pray reflectively and use their imaginations to encounter Jesus. As you lead the guided reflection, you may want to walk slowly around the room so that you can spot any misbehavior and gently correct it without interrupting the reflection.

This portion of the Reflect step may last anywhere from a minute with very young children to ten minutes with older children and adults.

Step Three: Allowing Quiet Time with God

To bring your guided reflection to a close, invite participants to spend time in silence with God, staying aware of God's presence. This is called contemplation. This last step may take anywhere from thirty seconds with young children to three or four minutes with older children and adults. To shape participants' quiet time with God, you might make use of the following.

Silent Prayer

Invite your participants to rest in God's presence. Stop talking and allow silence to enfold them. Gradually fade out the background music until there is total silence.

Transition

After an appropriate amount of time, offer a few gentle words to help participants transition back to the large group and the next activity. Invite them to open their eyes, sit up, stretch, and slowly and quietly return to their places.

Respect

Your participants' thoughts and reflections in prayer are theirs alone. You show respect for their conversation with God by letting them keep these thoughts to themselves. You can invite those who wish to share their experience to do so; however, do not require everyone to share. Some catechists use this time to have participants journal about their experience.

Resources for Leading Guided Reflections

Once you are familiar with the three steps outlined above, you will eventually become quite capable of formulating your own guided reflections, even spontaneously. It's not that different from making up a bedtime story—something parents, grandparents, aunts, uncles, and older siblings do all the time.

Until you get the hang of it, however, here are some resources I encourage you to look into.

Guided Reflections for Children, Volume 1: Praying with Scripture (Loyola Press, 2008)

Guided Reflections for Children, Volume 2: Praying My Faith (Loyola Press, 2008)

The Ball of Red String: A Guided Meditation for Children (Loyola Press, 2008)

Pray Me a Story Series 1 (Loyola Press, 2010)

Pray Me a Story Series 2 (Loyola Press, 2012)

The *Finding God: Our Response to God's Gifts* curriculum (grades 1–8), which includes guided reflections in every unit (Loyola Press, 2013)

In My Heart Room: 21 Love Prayers for Children (Liguori Publications, 1998)

Guided Meditations for Children: 40 Scripts and Activities Based on the Sunday Lectionary (Resource Publications, 1995; available as an ebook)

Journey to the Heart: Centering Prayer for Children (Paraclete Press, 2007)

Guided Meditations for Teens: Living Through the Church Year (Resource Publications, 1997; available as an ebook)

Learning to Meditate: A Thirty-Day Introduction to the Practice of Meditation (St. Mary's Press, 2000)

Guided Meditations for Child Catechumens (Resource Publications, 2000)

Guided Meditations for Adult Catechumens (Resource Publications, 1999; available as an ebook)

What Kids Are Saying About Reflective Prayer

I mentioned earlier that, for many kids, reflective prayer becomes their favorite part of the religious education experience. To support that assertion, here is some feedback from actual fourth graders that a catechist named Kim sent to my blog, *Catechist's Journey*. (Thank you, Kim!)

The thing I like most about our prayer times together is . . .

- When we meditate.
- Meditating because it gets me relaxed and thinking about Jesus.
- When we get to close our eyes and think about different times with Jesus.
- When Kim reads us stories and the time where she has us go to a place to spend time with Jesus.
- Talking about Jesus and closing our eyes to be with Jesus.
- I feel very connected with Jesus when we are there. I feel that he is in the room and praying with us to God.
- I get to be comfortable and think about God.
- That we relax and are able to think about God and Jesus.
- My favorite thing would be meditating.
- Closing our eyes and talking to Jesus for a while.

What I have learned about myself and my relationship with Jesus during our prayer times is . . .

- He is a very dear friend of mine.

- He saved me from sin.
- He loves me more than I thought.
- That we are all sons and daughters of Jesus, and Jesus is always open to talk to.
- I can count on Jesus to be there when I need him.
- I've learned Jesus is really close to me, and I will always love him.
- That he makes me feel special.
- Jesus has loved me no matter what I did, and he always will.
- That he is my friend.
- That I feel I'm a lot more close to Jesus, and I feel I actually belong here.

Additional comments:

- Praying with Kim is fun.
- I like praying.
- I wish I could do it all day every day.
- I love to go to prayer time with Kim. She is a great person to do this with, and I know God really loves her.

- I can't wait until the next time we pray again.
- The prayer time we had was really fun.
- Whenever our teacher says we are going to pray with Kim, we all get really excited to go and pray and be with Jesus.

An Example of a Guided Reflection

In case you're still wondering what an actual guided reflection looks like, here is an example taken from the *Finding God: Our Response to God's Gifts* Grade 5 Catechist Guide (Loyola Press).

Called to Holiness

Time: approximately 10 minutes

We all have imagination. Imagination allows us to go places and to do things that might otherwise be impossible. Today we are going to use imagination to help us pray. *(Pause.)*

Now, before we begin, find a position that feels most comfortable to you. *(Pause.)* If you like, close your eyes. *(Pause.)* Now relax your entire body—your neck . . . your shoulders . . . your arms . . . your legs. *(Pause.)* Feel all the tension flowing out of your body, into the air and away. *(Pause.)* Now be very still and listen to the rhythm of your breathing. Listen. *(Pause.)* Feel your breath go in and out, in and out, in and out. *(Pause.)* Now let's begin. *(Pause.)*

In your imagination see yourself in a place where you'd like to be. Maybe it's a place where you've met Jesus before, or maybe it's a different one. You can choose, because anything is possible in imagination. Why not make it your favorite time of year? *(Pause.)* Make the weather suit you today. *(Pause.)* Be there in your imagination. Wait for Jesus to join you. *(Pause.)*

He does, almost right away. As he comes in sight, you go to meet him. He's obviously glad to see you. Hear him tell you how glad he is to be with you again. *(Pause.)* As usual, he asks you what you were just doing. Sometimes your answer to that question would be, "Not much." But today it's different. He asks if you've been thinking about a verse from the Bible: "For I, the Lord, am your God; and you shall make and keep yourselves holy because I am holy."[*]

Now that's not your usual line of thought. But there's something in this verse that puzzles you. You don't have trouble with the idea of God being holy. But the idea of you being holy, of making and keeping yourself holy—well, that needs a little more explanation.

Perhaps Jesus asks you to think of qualities that you would use to describe God—maybe qualities such as loving,

---

[*] Leviticus 11:44

forgiving, patient, understanding, generous, and so on. Let's call these "God qualities." Then he asks you to think of someone you know who has some God qualities. Who is it? Tell Jesus about this person. *(Pause.)*

Jesus, a great storyteller himself, might ask you to share a story about this person. It may take some time to choose just one story, but that's OK. Take the time to remember and then share your story with Jesus. *(Pause.)*

Jesus explains that God is all-holy. He tells you that you are holy when you act in a God-like manner. When you live your life with generosity, understanding, and patience, then you are holy. Yes, you! You are holy.

What an awesome statement. Now think about that. *(Pause.)* Do you tell Jesus that being holy is what you want, but you're a little bit worried about being able to live up to that calling? *(Pause.)*

As usual, Jesus is reassuring. He wants you to know that you don't become holy all at once. You grow in holiness. You'll make mistakes, but that's OK. You can always learn from them and try again. He reminds you that the Holy Spirit is always with you to guide you. Jesus says that he himself will help you anytime you need him. *(Pause.)*

Does that make you feel better? *(Pause.)* Go with Jesus now deep down into your heart. You've discussed a lot with him already, so now just rest in his love. Words are no longer needed. Be still together. Know how much he cares for you. *(Pause.)*

You recognize that it's time to go now. If you want a special blessing from Jesus, just ask for it. Remember to thank him and then say good-bye. *(Pause.)*

Gradually bring yourself back to the room. *(Pause.)* Straighten up. *(Pause.)* Stretch. *(Pause.)* Plant your feet firmly on the floor. *(Pause.)* Look all around you. *(Pause.)* Everyone's here. We're all back.

Speaking to the Heart

Once, when I was teaching a four-week class on reflective prayer to a group of catechists, one of them became very enthused about the whole concept and couldn't wait to try it with her kids that week. When she returned to class the following week, she couldn't wait to tell the following story:

> I was substituting for a fifth-grade class and as the children arrived, I greeted them. One boy looked at me and asked, "Who are you?" I introduced myself and said that I was substituting. He said, "OK, but I don't believe in God!" I was caught off guard by such a bold and direct statement, but I chose not to deal with it at that moment. I said, "OK, thanks for telling me. Please have a seat." As the class went along, the boy was fine—not terribly interested but also not misbehaving. When it came time for prayer, I decided

to lead a guided reflection. I watched him closely throughout the experience as he followed directions. I couldn't tell what he was thinking about it all. When class was over, he lingered for a while and then came up to me and asked, "Are you going to be here next week?" I told him I would be. He said, "Good. Are we going to do this prayer thing again?" I said yes, and he replied, "Good," before turning to leave. I thought to myself, "As far as fifth-grade boys go, that was the equivalent of gushing!"

Indeed! For a fifth-grade boy to go out of his way first to claim he didn't believe in God and then to show interest in praying again next week is remarkable. The best thing about this story, however, is the fact that the catechist didn't debate the boy about the existence of God—which is probably what he was trying to goad her into. Instead, she led him to an encounter with God. Instead of speaking only to his head, she spoke to his heart. Now *that's* what the Reflect step is all about.

Now that you have led your participants through a prayerful encounter with the risen Lord, it is time to get them ready to return to the world with a new set of eyes.

Chapter 7

The RESPOND Step

10 Minutes

Remember how we talked about St. Ignatius's advice to "enter through their door but leave through your own"? The "leaving" time has come. In this step, you will send your participants through your door and back into the world with a new set of eyes—a new way of looking at life. These last few minutes of a session are an opportunity for you to review or summarize, assess how well your participants have grasped the Big Idea, invite your learners to practice a new behavior in the coming week, and, finally, send your participants forth with a prayerful attitude.

Assessment

Although we have been striving to make sure our faith formation resembles *Mass more than class*, catechesis does involve an academic component. It is a crucial part of our job as catechists to ensure that participants are acquiring a genuine knowledge of our faith and the ability to speak with gracious confidence about it. For this reason, it is a good idea to use these last few minutes of the session to summarize and review key concepts and to assess learners' grasp of them.

If you're having a hard time connecting assessment with faith formation, think about Jesus' own use of questioning as a way to gauge his disciples' understanding.

- "And he said, 'Are you also still without understanding?'" (Matthew 15:16)
- "And he said to them, 'Do you not understand this parable? How then will you understand all the parables?'" (Mark 4:13)
- "When he had washed their feet, and taken his garments, and resumed his place, he said to

them, 'Do you know what I have done to you?'" (John 13:12)

If we are going to teach as Jesus did, then we too need to assess whether our learners understand what we have presented to them. To assess (from the Latin word *assidere,* meaning "to sit with") is something we do *with* and *for* a learner, not *to* a learner. We assess not only our learners' comprehension of key concepts, but also our own effectiveness in communicating those concepts. We seek to assess the formation that is taking place in our learners and to offer feedback that leads to further growth.

Because people learn in a variety of ways, a variety of assessment formats is needed. Three of the most common types of assessment are formal (quizzes, tests, and essays), informal (observation of students' participation in classroom activities), and authentic (opportunities for participants to live what they've learned). Here's a little more about each type.

Formal Assessment

A formal assessment asks the question *What do you know or understand?* This type of assessment, accomplished in written or oral forms (usually quizzes and tests), is the most straightforward and provides the clearest feedback for you as a catechist. Be sure the items on your quizzes or tests are consistent with the learning outcomes for your lesson. Provide your learners with opportunities for self-assessment and give prompt feedback.

Informal Assessment

Informal assessment asks the question *What can you do with what you know, and how do you do it?* It can take two basic forms.

Ongoing

Assess your participants' grasp of concepts by observing their participation in discussions, group work, prayer/reflection, and service to others.

Specific Tasks

Include specific opportunities to evaluate verbal (oral and written) and nonverbal (drawn, crafted) expressions and responses.

The most common form of informal assessment is having learners complete the activity sheets or blackline masters that come with your catechist's manual or from your textbook publisher's Web site. As participants complete an activity sheet or blackline master, you can circulate around the room and assess whether individuals are grasping key concepts. You can also collect participants' work, take a look at it later, and provide feedback the next time you gather.

Another popular form of informal assessment is to have each participant share one thing he or she learned during the session. A catechist I know tells her learners that they can't leave until they've shared something substantive. Isn't it interesting how a little incentive like that can suddenly increase a young person's ability to recall and articulate?

Authentic Assessment

Authentic assessment is performance-based: it asks learners to put into action what they've learned. In many ways, this is the most effective type of assessment because it gives learners the opportunity to live out the call to discipleship. It also helps set a pattern for life.

Here are some ways to offer your participants an authentic assessment experience.

Service Experiences

Provide opportunities for your learners to put their faith into practice by serving others, either individually or as a group.

Assignments

Give your learners an assignment that requires them to practice a virtue or a corporal or spiritual work of mercy in the week to come. For example, one catechist I know was introducing his third-graders to the sacrament of reconciliation and focusing on the concept of forgiveness. He told his learners that between now and the next session, he wanted them to forgive someone who had done something wrong to them. The following week, as he introduced the Explore step of his session, he asked volunteers to share their experiences of forgiveness—and the stories were numerous and wonderful. When it comes to faith formation, homework should be less about reading and writing and more about *doing*.

Seeking Tangible Results

Like most people, catechists are eager to see tangible results from their work. This desire can sometimes lead catechists to rely on methods that "prove" their learners have memorized a set of cognitive principles. Although there is certainly a place in catechesis for quizzes and tests, assessment must also include a variety of methods that enable you to determine how successfully your participants are learning to live a Spirit-filled life.

Closing Prayer

You are now down to the last few minutes—or maybe seconds—of your faith formation session. Since your goal throughout has been to establish a prayerful climate, it makes sense that you would conclude the session with prayer—not a lengthy prayer service, but an opportunity for brief silent or communal time with God. I suggest you include the following:

1. A call to silence. (Pause for five seconds.)
2. The Sign of the Cross.
3. An invitation to join together in prayer.

Consider praying a traditional prayer that participants are expected to learn that year or one that is appropriate for the season. If young people are preparing for the sacrament of reconciliation, for example, it would make sense to pray the Act of Contrition. (You may need to provide the words for them at first.) During the season of Lent, consider praying the *Confiteor* from Mass, and during Easter, the *Gloria*. Or, to draw attention to May as the month of Mary, pray the Memorare. During October, the month of the holy Rosary, pray a decade of the Rosary.

4. An invitation to offer one another a sign of peace. (Remember: Mass more than class!)

5. The singing of a hymn that is appropriate to the season of the year—or simply its refrain.

6. An invitation to sign themselves with holy water as participants leave.

   As at the beginning of class, hold the bowl of holy water by the door as students exit, or have an aide or a reliable student do so.

Alternatively, you can bless students by signing their foreheads with the Sign of the Cross.

A simple closing prayer like this one will enable your participants to leave with a sense of the sacred as they go forth into the world. In ways we can't imagine, these holy words and actions shape us. They impact how we speak, how we behave, and how we interact with others and with God. By creating a climate of prayer and encouraging a sense of reverence throughout your session—by teaching the language of mystery—you have encouraged your participants to go forth in a spirit of prayer and reverence. You have helped them recognize the presence of Jesus in their midst.

And now you are sending them forth with a new set of eyes.

Chapter 8

Teaching Faith as a Second Language

Researchers from Northwestern University have shown that learning a second language acts as a "mental workout," fine-tuning the brain and increasing its ability to pay attention, process, and encode incoming information. Researchers have also shown that when people learn a second language, it changes the way they understand and speak their first language. Isn't that interesting?

But wait—there's more. Among other benefits, learning a second language does the following:

- Positively impacts intellectual growth
- Increases one's ability to think abstractly and creatively
- Enhances mental development

- Results in more flexible thinking and better listening skills
- Opens doors to communicate with others and to appreciate one's culture
- Removes barriers

All of this makes perfect sense when you think of faith formation as learning a second language—the language of mystery. As you may recall, the language of mystery involves more than just words. It relies on signs, symbols, images, rituals, actions, gestures, and song. When we teach faith as though we were teaching a second language, we increase not only the brainpower of our learners, but also their heart power.

As you may know, learning a second language is not easy. It is a struggle for many people. Nevertheless, people who learn to speak a second language often see their standard of living increase as they become capable of acquiring better jobs. Likewise, for many of those we teach, the language of faith—the language of mystery—is a foreign one. But by teaching them this language, we enable them to increase their spiritual standard of living by practicing the skills of forgiveness, prayer, and service to others. When we learn a second language, we become more capable of integrating ourselves into a new and different culture. When we learn the language of faith, we become capable of integrating ourselves into the "culture" of the kingdom of God.

Those who teach a second language know that the most effective approaches involve hands-on experience, visual aids, music and song, and other engaging activities—not just memorization. In fact, the most effective way to learn a second language is through immersion in that language. In the same way, our goal as catechists is not to teach a subject, but to immerse participants in the language of faith—the language of mystery that we speak and hear at Mass. We do this by teaching beyond the book, immersing them in our rich language of faith, the language of mystery that we "speak" when we worship at Mass. We don't just want them to dip their toes into it or be sprinkled by it. We want them to marinate in it.

In this book, I've offered some tips for meeting this goal. But when it comes right down to it, the best way to teach is to adapt strategies and techniques to your own style and circumstances. Be creative. Trust yourself and trust the Holy Spirit to guide you as you equip others to enter more deeply into the alternate reality that is the kingdom of God.

Acknowledgments

Many thanks to Arlene Astrowski and Most Holy Redeemer Parish in Evergreen Park, Illinois, for allowing me to practice my craft as a catechist and to try so many of the ideas that appear in this book. Thanks also to Loyola Press for providing me with the platform (my blog, www.catechistsjourney.com) from which I can dialogue with other catechists about all things catechetical, and to all the catechists whose ideas I have appropriated.

About the Author

Joe Paprocki is national consultant for faith formation at Loyola Press. He has thirty years of experience teaching at many different levels and continues to serve as a catechist. Paprocki is a popular speaker and the author of many books, including *Living the Mass* and *A Well-Built Faith*.

Also Available by Joe Paprocki

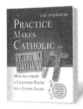

Practice Makes Catholic
$9.95 • 3322-7 • Pb

This is the perfect resource for all Catholics who want to get to the heart of what their faith is really about.

The Catechist's Toolbox
$9.95 • 2451-5 • Pb

This book of tips, techniques, and methodologies provides invaluable on-the-job training for new catechists.
Leader's Guide available!

Also in Spanish!

A Well-Built Faith
$9.95 • 2757-8 • Pb

From the Ten Commandments to the Trinity, this informative yet fun book helps Catholics know the facts about their faith. *Leader's Guide available!*

Also in Spanish!

The Bible Blueprint
$9.95 • 2898-8 • Pb

This nonthreatening introduction to God's Word uses a blueprint metaphor to help Catholics understand the basics of the Bible. *Leader's Guide available online!*

Also in Spanish!

All books are now available as eBooks. Visit www.loyolapress.com to purchase these other formats.

To order, call 800-621-1008 or visit www.loyolapress.com/toolbox